Other Books by Leland Gregory

Stupid
Conservatives

Weird and Wacky Tales
from the Right Wing

★ LELAND GREGORY ★

Andrews McMeel
Publishing, LLC

Kansas City • Sydney • London

Andrews McMeel Publishing, LLC
an Andrews McMeel Universal company
1130 Walnut Street, Kansas City, Missouri 64106

www.andrewsmcmeel.com

12 13 14 15 16 RR2 10 9 8 7 6 5 4 3 2 1

ISBN: 978-1-4494-0984-5

Library of Congress Control Number: 2011932642

Attention: Schools and Businesses
Andrews McMeel books are available at quantity discounts
with bulk purchase for educational, business,
or sales promotional use. For information, please e-mail the
Andrews McMeel Publishing Special Sales Department:
specialsales@amuniversal.com

Who's the Real Boob?

A woman in Hamilton, Ontario, who was breast-feeding her daughter in a swimming pool at a local public recreation center was ordered out of the pool by the lifeguard on duty. "I was sitting in the pool with my daughter in front of me, and I pulled down my bathing suit strap and took out my breast and put her on it," said the twenty-five-year-old mother. The lifeguard suggested the woman remove herself and the feeding child from the pool and go into a changing room. Authorities for the pool said the woman was breaking the recreation department's rule—not against indecent exposure, but for having "food or drink" in the pool. Sounds to me like the baby was just practicing his breaststroke.

In 1995, Dick Armey (R-TX) meant to speak about openly gay congressman Barney Frank (D-MA)—but somehow the words "Barney Fag" accidentally slipped out.

Two Sides
of Every Coin

"Who calls a shot like that? Who makes a decision like that? It's a disturbing trend."

★ Sarah Palin, West Allis, Wisconsin, November 6, 2009. Palin was promoting a conspiracy theory that the Obama administration had moved "In God We Trust" further to the edge of U.S. coins. The change was actually made during the Bush administration in 2007; Congress reversed the decision before Obama took office.

Close but No Cigar

When city officials in Edison, New Jersey, heard that the "Exxxotica Expo" had been booked at the New Jersey Convention and Exposition Center, they jumped into action to prevent the event from occurring. According to a November 5, 2009, article on the Huffington Post, the township council quickly amended its zoning laws to prohibit "any shows or sale of sexually oriented products in gatherings of 100 or more people at any place located within 1,000 feet of a place of public worship, school, playground, hospital or any child care center, or an area zoned for residential use." Only one problem—there are no places of public worship, schools, playgrounds, hospitals, child care centers, or areas zoned for residential use within 1,000 feet of the Expo Center, so the show went on as scheduled.

"I wanted to have all my ducks in a row so if we did get into a posture we could pretty much slam-dunk this thing and put it to bed."

★ Lee Cooke, mayor of Austin, 1991–97

Flu Me Once, Shame on You

"I find it interesting that it was back in the 1970s that the swine flu broke out under another—then under another Democrat president, Jimmy Carter. I'm not blaming this on President Obama. I just think it's an interesting coincidence."

★ Representative Michele Bachmann, April 28, 2009, on the 1976 swine flu outbreak that actually happened under Republican Gerald Ford's administration.

"My only regret with Timothy McVeigh is he did not go to the New York Times Building."

Ann Coulter, *New York Observer*, August 26, 2002. McVeigh's April 19, 1995, bomb attack destroyed the Alfred P. Murrah Federal Building in Oklahoma City, killing 168 people.

Pumping Irony

During the state's budget crisis in July 2008, and as a way to buy time for the legislature to pass a workable budget, California governor Arnold Schwarzenegger fired approximately ten thousand temporary and part-time workers and ordered that the salaries of two hundred thousand permanent employees be reduced to the minimum wage of $6.55 an hour. A week later, according to an August 8, 2008, article in the *Sacramento Bee*, State Controller John Chiang explained that the payrolls of the permanent employees could not be altered because they were written in the outdated COBOL computer language. He went on to explain that the only state employees still familiar with the antiquated code were the part-timers whose positions Schwarzenegger had just eliminated.

"I think it's very important for the American president to mean what he says. That's why I understand that the enemy could misread what I say. That's why I try to be as clearly I can."

★ George W. Bush, Washington, DC, September 23, 2004

I Don't Always Agree with My Opinions

Sometimes it seems like George W. Bush has short-term memory loss. We've all forgotten something at some point in time, such as our car keys or the children, but Bush has the ability to forget an entire ideological position. In an interview with ITV News on April 5, 2002, Bush said, "Far be it from the American president to get to decide who leads what country." Only a few minutes later, he said, "I made up my mind that Saddam needs to go."

Rim Shot

"Because you're going to see antihunting, anti–Second Amendment circuses from Hollywood, and here's how they do it: They use these delicate, tiny, very talented celebrity starlets; they use Alaska as a fund-raising tool for their anti–Second Amendment causes. Stand strong, and remind them patriots will protect our guaranteed, individual right to bear arms. And by the way, Hollywood needs to know, we eat, therefore we hunt."

★ Excerpt from Governor Sarah Palin's resignation speech,
Fairbanks, Alaska, July 26, 2009

Get Out and Push

In a *60 Minutes/Vanity Fair* poll, reported on October 2, 2011, just over half of Republicans (51 percent) correctly identified the meaning of "GOP" as "Grand Old Party" in a multiple-choice question. The second most popular choice, with 35 percent of the overall vote, was "Government of the People." "Grumpy Old People" received 7 percent of the vote; "God's Own Party" 3 percent; and 1 percent thought the abbreviation stood for "Gauntlet of Power."

"Guess what? Faisal Shahzad is a registered Democrat. I wonder if his SUV had an Obama sticker on it."

★ Rush Limbaugh, *The Rush Limbaugh Show*, May 4, 2010, discussing the failed Times Square car bomber, who was not registered to vote

What's on Your Mind?

"I'm thinking about killing Michael Moore, and I'm wondering if I could kill him myself, or if I would need to hire somebody to do it. . . . No, I think I could. I think he could be looking me in the eye, you know, and I could just be choking the life out. Is this wrong? I stopped wearing my What Would Jesus—band—Do, and I've lost all sense of right and wrong now. I used to be able to say, 'Yeah, I'd kill Michael Moore,' and then I'd see the little band: What Would Jesus Do? And then I'd realize, 'Oh, you wouldn't kill Michael Moore. Or at least you wouldn't choke him to death.' And you know, well, I'm not sure."

★ Glenn Beck, pondering the question
"What would people do for $50 million?" on
The Glenn Beck Program, May 17, 2005

Nutzis

Ann Coulter: "You will find liberals always rooting for savages against civilization."

Bill O'Reilly: "They didn't root for the Nazis against civilization."

Coulter: "Oh, yes they did. . . . It was only when Hitler invaded their precious Soviet Union that, at the last minute, they came in and suddenly started saying, 'Oh no, now you have to fight Hitler.'"

★ *The O'Reilly Factor*, May 7, 2010

"They intend to vote on the Sabbath, during Lent, to take away the liberty that we have right from God. This is an affront to God."

★ Representative Steve King (R-IA),
The Glenn Beck Program, March 18, 2010,
on Congress voting on the health-care bill

The Devil Is in the Details

Barbara Ann Radnofsky, a lawyer with more than twenty-five years of experience, claims that a twenty-two-word clause in a 2005 constitutional amendment to the Texas state constitution banning gay marriage inadvertently bans all marriage. The actual wording of the amendment reads as follows: "This state or a political subdivision of this state may not create or recognize any legal status identical or similar to marriage." Radnofsky claims that this constitutional amendment constitutes an "error of massive proportions" that "eliminates marriage in Texas," including common-law marriages. "You do not have to have a fancy law degree to read this and understand what it plainly says," said Radnofsky. According to a November 18, 2009, article in the *Fort Worth Star-Telegram*, a spokesman for Republican Greg Abbott, who drafted the amendment, wouldn't confirm or deny Radnofsky's claim.

"That cracker made a lot of African-American millionaires."

★ Rush Limbaugh, *The Rush Limbaugh Show*, July 13, 2010, on the death of longtime New York Yankees owner George Steinbrenner

A Very Queer Move

The U.S. Air Force spent an estimated $25 million training combat pilot Lieutenant Colonel Victor Fehrenbach, who served in Iraq, Afghanistan, and Kosovo, and was awarded nine air medals, including one for heroism during the 2003 invasion of Iraq. But according to a May 28, 2009, article in the *Dayton Daily News*, he was going to be discharged from the Air Force because he said he is gay. Fehrenbach, the son of military-officer parents, was born at Ohio's Wright-Patterson Air Force Base, and served the country for eighteen years, earning thirty awards and decorations with tours flying F-15Es. He was even one of the elite fighters enlisted to patrol the airspace over Washington, DC, on September 11, 2001. On December 22, 2010, President Barack Obama signed the law repealing the "don't ask, don't tell" policy. In January 2011, Fehrenbach was granted his request to end his twenty-year career with his rank and benefits intact.

Dissing Discourse

"She's a f—king raghead. We got a raghead in Washington; we don't need one in South Carolina. She's a raghead that's ashamed of her religion, trying to hide it behind being Methodist for political reasons." —South Carolina Republican state senator Jake Knotts, outside a Columbia bar on June 3, 2010, claiming one of the Republican candidates in the South Carolina governor's race, Nikki Haley, an Indian-American, had been set up by a network of Sikhs, and was programmed to run for governor by outside influences in foreign countries. Knotts later clarified his statement, saying it was "intended in jest."

"When I see a 9/11 victim family on television, or whatever, I'm just like, 'Oh, shut up.' I'm so sick of them because they're always complaining."

Glenn Beck, *The Glenn Beck Program*, September 9, 2005

Well, I'll Be a Monkey's Uncle

"You know what? Evolution is a myth. Why aren't monkeys still evolving into humans?"

★ Eventual Delaware Republican Senate candidate
Christine O'Donnell on Bill Maher's *Politically Incorrect*,
October 15, 1998

"I don't think we came from monkeys. I think that's ridiculous. I haven't seen a half-monkey, half-person yet."

★ Glenn Beck, *The Glenn Beck Program*, October 20, 2010

Setting Your Sights on Your Opponent

"I hope that's not where we're going, but, you know, if this Congress keeps going the way it is, people are really looking toward those Second Amendment remedies and saying, my goodness, what can we do to turn this country around? I'll tell you the first thing we need to do is take Harry Reid out."

★ Sharron Angle, Tea Party candidate and Nevada Republican Senate primary nominee, January 2010, touting the possibility of armed insurrection on *The Lars Larson Show*

"You know, we all have our inner demons. I, for one—I can't speak for you, but I'm on the verge of moral collapse at any time. It can happen by the end of the show."

★ Glenn Beck, *The Glenn Beck Program*,
November 6, 2006

Booze It and Lose It

Mike Krusee of Austin was arrested and charged with driving while intoxicated in late April 2008. His personalized license plate had expired, and he failed a field sobriety test but claimed to have had only one glass of wine. Under the newly enacted "driver responsibility program," Krusee, if convicted, could have faced 180 days in jail and a $4,000 fine—including at least $1,000 in extra fines for first-time drunk drivers. What's odd about this story, according to a May 1, 2008, article in the *Austin American-Statesman*, is that the law was written by Krusee himself as the chairman of the Texas House Transportation Committee and a member of the Texas House Judiciary Committee. A judge eventually dismissed the charges against Krusee.

★ ★ ★

George W. Bush presided over the execution of 152 prisoners, more than any other governor in U.S. history.

Open Mouth, Insert Foot

"She's either Puerto Rican, or the same thing as Cuban—I mean they are all very hot. They have the, you know, part of the black blood in them and part of the Latino blood in them that together makes it."

★ Governor Arnold Schwarzenegger, March 3, 2006, on California's only Latina Republican, Assemblywoman Bonnie Garcia

"Nothing is more important in the face of a war than cutting taxes."

Tom DeLay, March 12, 2003, speaking at an America's Community Bankers meeting

The President and the Professor

Sit back and enjoy the comic stylings of President George W. Bush and economic adviser Dr. Jeffrey Brown, as they perform their classic routine "C is for Student":

George W. Bush (March 10, 2005): Now, I've asked Jeff Brown to join us today, PhD. Yes. I'm a C student. He's the PhD. He's the adviser. I'm the president. What does that tell you? It tells you there's hope for all you C students out there.

Dr. Jeffrey Brown: I'm a PhD in economics, and I'm a professor at one of the other great midwestern universities.

Bush (March 14, 2005): PhD in economics. It's an interesting lesson, isn't it? He's the adviser and the PhD. I'm the president and a fair student.

Bush (May 19, 2005): I like to remind people, he's a PhD, and I was a C student. I want you to take note of who's the president and who's the adviser.

Better Than a Poke in the Eye

Reacting to an article they read in a January 2008 issue of the London newspaper the *Sun*, Oklahoma state senators rushed through legislation to ban the dangerous practice about which they read. Senate Bill 844 was filed by Oklahoma state senator Cliff Branan, and eventually passed on April 21, 2009. What was the frightening new practice that the senators needed to protect their citizenry against? Tattooing a design in ink into the white part of the eyeball known as the sclera. "If we can stop . . . one person from doing it, we've been successful," said Branan. According to a February 20, 2009, report on KSBI-TV in Oklahoma City, a local tattoo artist said the law was useless because "common sense" would stop most people from getting the procedure.

"[This is] a place that would be pretty much like the place that I would have grown up in, I think, if I had grown up here."

★ Alan Keyes, 2004, on the Chicago neighborhood he moved to in order to qualify as a candidate for U.S. Senate in Illinois

Who Stole My Cheese?

Ham and cheese are two things that go together, so it was only natural that when cheese was in trouble, ham was there to bail it out. What am I talking about? Well, the cheese is the Cuba Cheese Museum in Cuba, New York, and the ham comes in the form of pork-barrel spending. In 2005, New York governor George Pataki criticized the legislature for spending money on ridiculous pet projects like cheese museums, but the cheese museum he referenced wasn't the one that received $5,000 in April 2006 from a fund controlled by Governor Pataki himself—the other one was. And since there are two cheese museums in New York, it's only fair that the state cut the cheese money between them—because what's Gouda for one cheese museum is Gouda for the other.

"We pick up stray animals and spay them. These mothers need to be spayed if they can't take care of their [children]."

Charleston City, South Carolina, councilman Larry Shirley, *Charleston Post and Courier*, September 29, 2006, on his solution to the city's youth crime problem

The Race Chase

"This president I think has exposed himself over and over again as a guy who has a deep-seated hatred for white people or the white culture. . . . I'm not saying he doesn't like white people, I'm saying he has a problem. This guy is, I believe, a racist."

★ Glenn Beck on President Obama,
The Glenn Beck Program, July 28, 2009

"I even accept for the sake of argument that sexual orgies eliminate social tensions and ought to be encouraged."

★ Supreme Court justice Antonin Scalia, Harvard University, *Harvard Crimson*, September 29, 2004

I'll Be Back

"If I would do another *Terminator* movie I would have Terminator travel back in time and tell Arnold not to have a special election."

★ California governor Arnold Schwarzenegger, November 10, 2005, concerning the special election he called in which all four of his ballot initiatives were soundly defeated

Thad Cochran (R-MS), Senate Appropriations Committee ranking member, inserted a piece of legislation in the 2010 federal budget earmarking $500,000 for the University of Southern Mississippi for cannabis eradication research. That's a real buzz kill.

Flip-Flop

He seemed like a shoo-in for the simple reason that he ran unopposed, but James Epperson of Edwards County, Texas, was ruled ineligible to serve in the position of county commissioner. Apparently, Epperson had violated the state election law when he voted in the Democratic primary, and was therefore not allowed to run for a seat in the 2000 Republican primary.

"I guarantee it's one of their long-term goals, to have one sort of borderless mass continent."

★ Rand Paul, Kentucky GOP Senate nominee and Tea Party favorite, May 25, 2010, on the future of North America

Please Spay
or Neuter

"My grandmother was not a highly educated woman, but she told me as a small child to quit feeding stray animals. You know why? Because they breed. You're facilitating the problem if you give an animal or a person ample food supply. They will reproduce, especially ones that don't think too much further than that. And so what you've got to do is you've got to curtail that type of behavior. They don't know any better."

★ South Carolina lieutenant governor Andre Bauer,
January 24, 2010, comparing stray animals to
lower-income residents who rely on
government subsidies such as food stamps
and free school lunches

"If Obamacare passes, that free insurance card that's in people's pockets is gonna be as worthless as a Confederate dollar after the War Between the States— the Great War of Yankee Aggression."

★ Representative Paul Broun (R-GA), March 18, 2010

The Right Man for the Job

"A lot of people don't realize that the vice president is really a creature of the Senate. My paycheck actually comes from the Senate. And all that goes back to when they wrote the Constitution, and they created the post of vice president, and they got down to the end of the Constitutional Convention and suddenly realized they hadn't given him anything to do—didn't have any real work. So they said, well, we'll make him the presiding officer of the Senate."

★ Vice President Dick Cheney, at a March 22, 2005, town hall meeting on Social Security in Reno, Nevada

"I think, on a national level, your Department of Law there in the White House would look at some of the things that we've been charged with and automatically throw them out."

★ Sarah Palin, ABC News interview, July 7, 2009, referring to a governmental department that does not exist

Keeping Abreast of Politics

According to a February 7, 2005, *Washington Post* article, during a Senate Judiciary Committee discussion about class-action lawsuits and silicone breast implants, Oklahoma state representative, physician, and Southern Baptist deacon Tom Coburn (who is known as "Dr. No" for his tendency to place holds on and vote against bills he views as unconstitutional) said, "I thought I would just share with you what science says today about silicone breast implants. If you have them, you're healthier than if you don't. That is what the ultimate science shows. . . . In fact, there's no science that shows that silicone breast implants are detrimental and, in fact, they make you healthier." Finally, the proof men have been waiting on for years.

"If you are not electing Christians, then, in essence, you are going to legislate sin."

Representative Katherine Harris (R-FL), *Florida Baptist Witness*, August 24, 2006

Bumper Sticker Philosophy

"We have brave men and women who are willing to step forward because they know what's at stake. They're willing to sacrifice their lives for this great country. What I'm asking all of you tonight is not to put on a uniform. Put on a bumper sticker. Is it that much to ask? Is it that much to ask to step up and serve your country?"

★ Senator Rick Santorum (R-PA), January 2006, urging supporters to serve their country by putting a Rick Santorum bumper sticker on their cars

"I have no problem with homosexuality— I have a problem with homosexual acts."

★ Senator Rick Santorum (R-PA), April 7, 2003, clarifying earlier remarks in which he equated homosexuality with incest and bestiality

tedstevens@ compuserve.com

We've all heard the claim that Congress is out of touch with reality, and even if I wanted to disprove this statement it would be technically impossible with statements like this: "The Internet is not something you just dump something on. It's not a truck. It's a series of tubes. And if you don't understand, those tubes can be filled, and if they are filled, when you put your message in, it gets in line, and it's going to be delayed by anyone that puts into that tube enormous amounts of material."

★ Senate Commerce Committee chairman Ted Stevens (R-AK), who was in charge of regulating the Internet, explaining how that dang-fool Internet really worked, during a congressional debate on June 28, 2006

The Pot Calling the Kettle Black

"It doesn't look like Michelle Obama follows her own nutritionary dietary advice. And then we hear that she's out eating ribs at 1,500 calories a serving with 141 grams of fat.... No, I'm trying to say that our First Lady does not project the image of women that you might see on the cover of the *Sports Illustrated* swimsuit issue, or of a woman Alex Rodriguez might date every six months, or what have you."

★ Rush Limbaugh, *The Rush Limbaugh Show*,
February 21, 2011

"These were highly civil comments, for crying out loud. I mean, people are going nuts. *USA Today*, the Politico. And some people were suggesting that my comments were below the belt. Well, take a look at some pictures. Given where she wears her belts—I mean, she wears them high up there around the bust line. Isn't just about everything about her below the belt when you look at the fashion sense she has?"

★ Rush Limbaugh, *The Rush Limbaugh Show*, February 22, 2011, defending his statement about First Lady Michelle Obama's weight

I Might Not Know Art, but I Know What I Don't Like

Chicago, Illinois, Eleventh Ward alderman James Balcer was appalled by an outdoor mural on a wall that he claimed was a "threat to the community" as it "could have" created a "gang problem." The alderman couldn't say exactly why he thought that because "I don't know what all the gang affiliations are." Balcer ordered the city's "Graffiti Blasters" team to paint over it. Turns out that the mural was not only on private property, but it was also a commissioned artwork by well-known Chicago artist and muralist Gabriel Villa. According to a May 20, 2009, article on the Huffington Post, Balcer, not to be deterred, defended his decision by saying he was justified because "everything in it was death."

"We have not
failed in Iraq.
. . . The president
understands that
we need to have
a way forward
in Iraq that is
more successful."

Bush national security adviser
Stephen Hadley, December 4, 2006

Full-Court Press

Katie Couric: "What other Supreme Court decisions do you disagree with?"

Sarah Palin: "Well, let's see. There's—of course—in the great history of America rulings, there have been rulings, there's never going to be absolute consensus by every American. And there are—those issues, again, like *Roe v. Wade,* where I believe are best held on a state level and addressed there. So, you know—going through the history of America, there would be others, but—"

Couric: "Can you think of any?"

Palin: "Well, I could think of—of any, again, that could be best dealt with on a more local level. Maybe I would take issue with. But you know, as mayor, and then as governor, and even as a vice president, if I'm so privileged to serve, wouldn't be in a position of changing those things but in supporting the law of the land as it reads today."

★ CBS News interview, October 1, 2008

The Cycle of Mishaps

The third time wasn't a charm for President George W. Bush when he fell off his bike and collided with a local police officer in Gleneagles, Scotland. It was the third time that Bush had wiped out: The first time, he flew over the handlebars of his mountain bike while on his ranch in Texas, and the second time was in 2003, when he somehow fell off a self-balancing Segway. The president suffered "mild to moderate" scrapes on his hands and arms, but was thankfully wearing his helmet at the time, because, as White House spokesman Scott McClellan said, it was raining lightly that day. The Scottish policeman suffered a "very minor" ankle injury, but it was Bush and his bicycle that rode back in a Secret Service vehicle.

I Did Not Know That

"Reports that say that something hasn't happened are always interesting to me, because, as we know, there are known knowns; there are things we know we know. We also know there are known unknowns; that is to say we know there are some things we do not know. But there are also unknown unknowns, the ones we don't know we don't know. And if one looks throughout the history of our country and other free countries, it is the latter category that tend to be the difficult ones."

★ Secretary of Defense Donald Rumsfeld, Department of Defense press briefing, February 12, 2002

A Real Stretch

A story in the June 25, 2006, *Lexington Herald-Leader* reported that Kentucky governor Ernie Fletcher was chauffeured to work every day in a limousine. The governor claimed he needed the taxpayer-funded limousine and driver for security reasons, and not because he's lazy—even though the total distance from where he lived to where he worked was a mere five hundred feet. At the same time the governor got his free daily rides, his administration was promoting a statewide fitness initiative encouraging Kentuckians to walk or bike more. Whatever the reason Fletcher had for being driven to work—fear or laziness—it answered the age-old riddle: Why did the governor cross the road? To get his limo to the other side.

"I talk to those who've lost their lives, and they have that sense of duty and mission."

★ Senator Jeff Sessions (R-AL), at Robert Gates's confirmation hearing for U.S. secretary of defense on December 5, 2006, discussing American casualties in the Iraq War

Pro-Choice

"If they want to be a homosexual or bisexual when they turn eighteen, that's fine and good. But I think we ought to wait until they're of age. They're at their vulnerable times—nine, ten, eleven, twelve—when they're trying to find out their sexuality . . . and we're exposing them to this; and the studies show that if they're exposed to it there's a greater percentage of them that would be homosexual or bisexual."

★ Texas Republican state senator Robert Talton, explaining that choosing to be gay when you're of legal age is "fine and good," but allowing gays and lesbians to become foster parents might unduly affect a young person's "choice." His amendment, prohibiting gay foster parents from adopting, failed.

On the Government Dole

Washington state senator Joe Zarelli admitted to the *Columbian* newspaper in September 2002 that he had collected $12,000 in unemployment benefits in 2001–02 while simultaneously being paid $32,000 a year as a senator, which he didn't report. Zarelli claimed he "had no clue" he was supposed to divulge his legislator's salary, and he blamed the Employment Security Department for not discovering his mistake and explaining why what he was doing was illegal. Zarelli went on to say he thought he was being targeted by the agency not because he was cheating on his unemployment benefits but because he was a Republican. In Zarelli's defense, with the small amount of work state senators do, I can understand why he might consider himself unemployed.

"I *am* the federal government."

Tom DeLay (R-TX), May 14, 2003, to the owner of Ruth's Chris Steak House, after being told to put out his cigar because federal regulations banned smoking in the building

GOP Pride

Mike Taylor, former salon owner and 2002 Republican U.S. Senate candidate from Montana, bitterly withdrew from the race in October, citing the fact that his Democratic opponent ran attack ads that Taylor claimed made him look gay. Guess his opponent pointed out that Taylor was a former salon owner, and people made up their own minds.

Senator Richard "Dick" Lugar (R-IN) sponsored a bill in October 2005 to rename the Crowne Plaza federal building in Kingston, Jamaica, the Colin L. Powell Residential Plaza.

A Break
in the Action

During the U.N. World Summit on September 14, 2005, President George W. Bush was seen hurriedly scribbling down a note and handing it to Secretary of State Condoleezza Rice. Was it a vital communiqué concerning terrorist activity, or maybe the phone number of someone he wanted tapped? No, it was a note asking permission to go to the little president's room. The note, with its bad punctuation and unorthodox upper/lowercase lettering, read: "I think I may NEED A BATHroom break? Is this possi[ble]. W." The story and note were somehow leaked to the press.

Second in Command

"[T]hey're in charge of the U.S. Senate, so if they want to they can really get in there with the senators and make a lot of good policy changes that will make life better for Brandon and his family and his classroom."

★ Sarah Palin, interview with NBC affiliate KUSA-TV in Colorado, October 21, 2008, incorrectly explaining the vice president's constitutional role after being asked by a third-grader what the vice president does.

"As for that VP talk all the time, I'll tell you, I still can't answer that question until somebody answers for me what is it exactly that the VP does every day."

★ Sarah Palin, before U.S. presidential candidate John McCain chose her as his vice-presidential running mate, during an interview on CNBC's *Kudlow & Company*, July 31, 2008

A Real Feminazi

"The feminist agenda is not about equal rights for women. It is about a socialist, antifamily political movement that encourages women to leave their husbands, kill their children, practice witchcraft, destroy capitalism, and become lesbians."

★ Pat Robertson, fund-raising letter, 1992

"Sometimes, you know, I consider myself, too, as a feminist, whatever that means."

★ Sarah Palin, interview with Greta Van Susteren, *On the Record*, November 10, 2008

The Dog Trot

President Bush has been accused of dropping the ball before, but on September 2, 2003, he was accused of dropping the dog. Before boarding Air Force One in Waco, Texas, for their trip back to Washington, First Lady Laura Bush and President Bush were greeting members of the Midway All-Stars, a Waco-area Little League girls softball team that had recently won the world championship. The girls were introduced to Barney, the Bush's black Scottish terrier, and were smiling and waving to the little pooch as Mrs. Bush handed the dog to her husband. Their innocent faces quickly turned to horror and disbelief when the president fumbled the pass-off and Barney tumbled out of his hands and landed headfirst on the tarmac. The dog was unhurt, and for some reason Dick Cheney was whisked away to an undisclosed location.

Le Page Out of Le Book

"Quite frankly, the science that I'm looking at says there is no [problem]," said Governor Paul LePage of Maine, in discussing the possible effects of Bisphenol A (BPA), commonly used in plastics. "There hasn't been any science that identifies that there is a problem." LePage then added, "The only thing that I've heard is if you take a plastic bottle and put it in the microwave and you heat it up, it gives off a chemical similar to estrogen. So the worst case is some women may have little beards."

★ Reported in the *Bangor Daily News*,
February 22, 2011

Sum Dum Ho

During a House Elections Committee meeting discussing voter-identification legislation, Texas Republican state representative Betty Brown suggested a solution to the confusion caused by Chinese-Americans Anglicizing their names (which yields nonstandard spellings): "Rather than everyone here having to learn Chinese—I understand it's a rather difficult language—do you think that it would behoove you and your citizens to adopt a name that we could deal with more readily here?" According to an April 8, 2009, article in the *Houston Chronicle*, Brown went on to ask Ramey Ko, a representative of the Organization of Chinese Americans, "Can't you see that this is something that would make it a lot easier for you and the people who are poll workers if you could adopt a name just for identification purposes that's easier for Americans to deal with?"

Stuck in the Headlights

The studio bustled with activity. Lights were focused as cameras rolled into position. Representative Martin Hoke (R-OH) was preparing to comment on Bill Clinton's 1994 State of the Union address. This was his big moment. A young female producer placed a microphone on the representative and then walked behind him to make sure the transmitter was on. With the producer's back to him, Representative Hoke turned to a fellow House member, cupped his hands in front of his chest, and said, "She has the beeg breasts." Of course, Representative Hoke didn't know the director was doing a camera check and the camera was on and running the entire time. Now who's the bigger boob?

Here's a little more tit for tat about Representative Hoke. He made clear the reason he came to Washington was not for his political career but for his social life. "I could date [newly elected congresswomen] Maria Cantwell or Blanche Lambert—they're hot," Hoke said to the *New York Times*. With members like Hoke, it should have been called the "Frat House of Representatives."

Serious Pork-Barrel Legislation

Missouri Republican senators Kit Bond and Jim Talent and Republican representative Jo Ann Emerson announced on November 23, 2004, that they had earmarked federal money for three-dozen projects in southern Missouri, including $50,000 for wild-hog control.

"Now, tell me the truth, boys, is this kind of fun?"

★ House majority leader Tom Delay (R-TX), September 9, 2005, at the Astrodome in Houston, Texas, speaking to three young hurricane evacuees from New Orleans

The Devil Made Me Do It

"It may be a blessing in disguise. . . . Something happened a long time ago in Haiti, and people might not want to talk about it. Haitians were originally under the heel of the French. You know, Napoleon the Third, or whatever. And they got together and swore a pact to the devil. They said, 'We will serve you if you will get us free from the French.' True story. And so, the devil said, 'OK, it's a deal.' Ever since, they have been cursed by one thing after the other."

★ Pat Robertson, January 13, 2010, blaming the devil
for the earthquake in Haiti that destroyed the capital
and killed tens of thousands of people

All There in Black and White

"[Obama] wouldn't have been voted president if he weren't black. Somebody asked me over the weekend why does somebody earn a lot of money have a lot of money, because she's black. It was Oprah. No, it can't be. Yes, it is. There's a lot of guilt out there—show we're not racists, we'll make this person wealthy and big and famous and so forth. . . . If Obama weren't black he'd be a tour guide in Honolulu, or he'd be teaching Saul Alinsky constitutional law, or lecturing on it in Chicago."

★ Rush Limbaugh, *The Rush Limbaugh Show*, July 6, 2010. Saul Alinsky is generally considered the founder of modern community organizing.

A Double Dose of Trouble

Texas state representative Joe Driver, who promotes his opposition to the "big spending habits of liberals in government" on his Web site, was discovered to have been routinely double-billing the government for travel expenses. The eighteen-year house veteran seemed surprised when a reporter for The Associated Press explained that the practice of double-dipping was illegal. Wrote The Associated Press in an August 16, 2010, article: "Driver insists he thought the double-billing was perfectly appropriate—until talking about it with the AP," at which point he appeared to change his mind. "Well, it doesn't sound [appropriate] now [if] you bring it up that way," he admitted. "[To learn that] pretty well screws my week."

Hero Today—
Gone Tomorrow

As reported in a May 1, 2008, article in the *Washington Post*, army medic Monica Brown was awarded the Silver Star for bravery after putting herself in imminent danger in order to treat wounded American soldiers in Afghanistan. Two days after her heroic and selfless actions, she was ordered home against her own protest. Apparently, some generals felt nervous that a female appeared to be "in combat," which is a violation of army rules.

Good Grief

"Ok, so, this is total crap, we sit the kids down to watch 'The Charlie Brown Christmas Special' and our muslim president is there, what a load . . . try to convince me that wasn't done on purpose," stated the Facebook diatribe of Russell Wiseman, the mayor of Arlington, Tennessee. Wiseman, who was outraged that President Barack Obama preempted the annual telecast of the 1965 special *A Charlie Brown Christmas* to speak on the war in Afghanistan went on to write that Obama had "deliberately timed" his remarks about the war so that it would block the religious *Peanuts* message. According to a December 4, 2009, article in the *Memphis Commercial Appeal*, Wiseman (obviously not one mentioned in the Bible) added, "You obama people need to move to a muslim country . . . oh wait, that's America . . . pitiful" and "you know, our forefathers had it written in the original Constitution that ONLY property owners could vote, if that has stayed in there, things would be different."

A Real Pain in the Butt

According to a December 30, 2008, article in the *Des Moines Register*, Iowa state representative Darrell Hanson unsuccessfully took up the torch left behind by state senator Willard Hansen to remove language from Section 1A.1 of the state's constitution. The poorly phrased passage, which describes the state seal, reads: "citizen soldier, with a plow in his rear, supporting the American flag and liberty cap with his right hand, and his gun with his left." Hanson said, "Willard always felt sorry for the poor guy described as 'the citizen soldier, with a plow in his rear,' but his attempts to change that language to 'with a plow behind him' never went anywhere."

Trying to Get Your Goat

"I made a personal commitment last year to make sure the house would criminalize that type of disgusting, barbaric behavior," said Republican Adam Hasner, majority leader for Florida's house of representatives. According to a May 7, 2010, article in the *Miami Herald*, legislators were trying to make sex with animals illegal in Florida, but their colleagues across the aisle didn't find the issue to be of paramount importance—there have been very few cases of sexual battery upon an animal—and therefore wouldn't debate the bill. "[Democrats] just don't like to discuss sex and animals," confirmed Democratic representative Jim Waldman.

Getting the Shaft

On February 19, 2002, George W. Bush was invited by the prime minister of Japan, Junichiro Koizumi, to a religious ceremony called a *yabusame*. In this ceremonial archery event, which dates from the sixth century, mounted archers shoot at three stationary targets while riding at full gallop. The warriors are in deep meditation during the event, and each arrow is accompanied by a prayer for peace and abundant harvest. Throughout the ceremony, President Bush was heard exclaiming "Yeah!" after every successful arrow strike.

Suffer the Little Children

Virginia state legislator Bob Marshall voiced his opposition to spending state money for Planned Parenthood by claiming that the organization is partly responsible for the number of disabled children in America. "The number of children who are born subsequent to a first abortion with handicaps has increased dramatically," Marshall said. "Why? Because when you abort the firstborn of any, nature takes its vengeance on the subsequent children." Marshall went on to explain his biblical reference: "In the Old Testament, the firstborn of every being, animal, and man was dedicated to the Lord." According to a February 22, 2010, article in the *Richmond News Leader*, Marshall said the organization should rename itself "Planned Barrenhood."

Two-Stepping

On March 9, 2010, Candy Crowley of CNN's *State of the Union* interviewed former House Republican leader and *Dancing with the Stars* participant Tom DeLay shortly after the Senate had heard a proposal for unanimous consent for the extension of unemployment insurance.

DeLay: "There is an argument to be made that these extensions, the unemployment benefits, keep people from going and finding a job. In fact, there are some studies that have been done that show people stay on unemployment compensation and they don't look for a job until two or three weeks before they know the benefits are going to run out."

Crowley: "People are unemployed because they want to be?"

DeLay: "Well, it is the truth. And people in the real world know it."

And on *That* Note

Chairman of the Florida Republican Party Jim Greer had a continuous procession of emergency "notes" delivered to him during a Republican National Committee meeting. According to an April 17, 2010, article in the *Orlando Sentinel*, the "notes" were all blank. A Florida RNC official concluded that Greer was simply trying to make himself appear important to his colleagues. Following his arrest on June 2, 2010, after being indicted on six felony counts related to raiding the state party's treasury, Greer could pass notes to his fellow inmates.

Not the Man
He Used to Be

According to a June 4, 2010, article in the *Chicago Sun-Times*, former U.S. representative and current senator Mark Kirk (R-IL) frequently used "swagger and braggadocio in talking about his 21 years of military service" as qualification for office. Soon, his house of cards began to tumble, and Kirk explained, "I simply misremembered it wrong." Although he touted his faux qualifications frequently, apparently Kirk simply "misremembered" that he was not actually "in" the Desert Storm war; did not actually "command the Pentagon War Room" when he was assigned there as a navy reservist; and was not actually once naval "Intelligence Officer of the Year."

The Island of Misfit Toys

Republican Douglas Hughes proposed several "out of the box" ideas in his 2010 run for governor of California, including building a "triple fence" along California's border with Mexico, granting immigrants a green-card reward system, and allowing the state to sell drugs to addicts for half price. And when it came to solving the state's child-molestation problem, Hughes had a doozy of an idea. According to a May 21, 2010, article in the *Daily Caller*, he suggested developing an island thirty miles off the Santa Barbara coast to contain the state's pedophiles, who would "write their own constitution, build their own infrastructure, and maintain a society."

According to his campaign Web site, "The first of the pedophiles to go to the island would be a lead team for 'their society' such as police, fire personnel, judges, fish and game agents, forest rangers, ranchers, farmers, building contractors, surveyors, and the like to establish the 'island community. This lead team will be responsible for creating a master plan for the 'Island.'" One other rule: No kids allowed.

Which witch?

"I dabbled into witchcraft—I never joined a coven. But I did, I did . . . I dabbled into witchcraft. I hung around people who were doing these things. I'm not making this stuff up. I know what they told me they do. . . . One of my first dates with a witch was on a satanic altar, and I didn't know it. I mean, there's a little blood there and stuff like that. We went to a movie and then had a midnight picnic on a satanic altar."

★ 2010 Delaware GOP Senate candidate
Christine O'Donnell on Bill Maher's
Politically Incorrect, October 29, 1999

"I'm not a witch. . . . I'm you."

★ Christine O'Donnell in an October 4, 2010,
TV commercial trying to debunk the rumor
that she was a witch

He Just Misspoke

Dan Maes, 2010 Republican candidate for governor of Colorado, began his campaign supporting "green" programs, such as Denver's "bike-sharing" project (which is exactly what it sounds like), but he soon started backpedaling. According to an August 4, 2010, article in the *Denver Post*, Maes now believes that such progressive projects are, in fact, plots. "(I)f you do your homework and research, you realize that [encouraging people to ride bikes instead of driving their cars] is part of a greater strategy to rein in American cities under a United Nations treaty."

The Penal Code

The only state that still has a ban on selling sex toys is . . . Alabama (surprise!). However, the buzz was that Pleasures: One Stop Romance Shop in Huntsville had expanded its business by moving into a former bank building in order to use the three drive-up windows to sell condoms and dildos to go. According to a November 9, 2010, article in the *Huntsville Times*, the business is getting around the state law, which prohibits the sale unless used for "bona fide medical, scientific, educational, legislative, judicial, or law enforcement purposes," by simply having customers provide a brief written description of their "legitimate" conditions in order to make a purchase.

People Are Strange, When You're a Stranger

As one of his final acts in office, outgoing Florida governor Charlie Crist signed a pardon exonerating a singer following an infamous arrest for exposing himself to a crowd during a concert. According to a November 17, 2010, article on the Huffington Post, Crist said, "There's some troubling aspects to it as to whether there was a valid conviction. The more I learn about it, the more I'm convinced a wrong may have been done here. My heart just bleeds for his legacy and his family." So after nearly forty-one years, Jim Morrison of the Doors (who died in 1971) has been officially forgiven for his 1969 charge of indecent exposure at a concert at the Dinner Key Auditorium in Miami. I guess the time to hesitate was through.

On December 23, 2003, New York governor George Pataki pardoned Lenny Bruce, infamous groundbreaking comedian, who had died from a heroin overdose thirty-seven years earlier. "They call it the Halls of Justice because the only place you get justice is in the halls."

★ Lenny Bruce

A Real Dope

"Drug use, some might say, is destroying this country. And we have laws against selling drugs, pushing drugs, using drugs, importing drugs. . . . And so if people are violating the law by doing drugs, they ought to be accused, and they ought to be convicted, and they ought to be sent up."

★ Rush Limbaugh, *Rush Limbaugh* television show, October 5, 1995

"I am addicted to prescription pain medication."

★ Rush Limbaugh, *The Rush Limbaugh Show*, October 10, 2003

A Real
Tongue Lashing

Naples, Florida, city councilman Fred Tarrant was outraged over Ted Lay's *Famous Tongue Mona Al Monica* painting (which shows side-by-side impressions of the *Mona Lisa*, Albert Einstein, and Monica Lewinsky sticking out their tongues) and demanded it be removed from its place at a Naples municipal art center. Tarrant thought the painting was obscene because Lewinsky's "tongue" resembled a penis, which the artist denied. According to an August 11, 2001, *Naples Daily News* report, the councilman relied on the opinions of "advisers" to formulate his opinion of the penis-shaped tongue because Tarrant is, in fact, blind.

Developing Farmland

According to a February 23, 2011, article in the *Florida Tribune*, the state legislature had introduced Florida Senate Bill 1246, which would make it a first-degree felony to take photographs of any farmland, even if the photographer is on public land, without the express written permission of the land's owner. The purpose behind the bill is somewhat of a mystery, but it is assumed it is a preemptive measure to ward off campaigns by People for the Ethical Treatment of Animals.

Don't Cry For Me, Argentina

After being out of his office for several days and repeated calls brought forth the excuse from his staff that he was "hiking the Appalachian Trail," South Carolina governor Mark Sanford, it turned out, had actually been chasing some Argentine tail. Sanford admitted, after being discovered in Hartsfield-Jackson Atlanta International Airport, that he had been having an extramarital affair with a woman in Buenos Aires. According to a June 24, 2009, CNN.com report, Sanford admitted the affair to reporters, in a strangely suggestive way, saying, "I'm a bottom-line kind of guy. I'll lay it out, it's going to hurt, and we'll let the chips fall as they may."

Physician Cure Thyself

"He is exaggerating the effects of the disease. He's moving all around and shaking, and it's purely an act. . . . This is really shameless of Michael J. Fox. Either he didn't take his medication or he's acting, one of the two."

★ Rush Limbaugh, *The Rush Limbaugh Show*, October 23, 2006, on an ad endorsing Democrat Claire McCaskill (who supports embryonic stem-cell research) for U.S. Senate by Michael J. Fox, who has been diagnosed with Parkinson's disease

Representative J. Gresham Barrett (R-SC) held a "Shag 'n' Eat" fund-raiser in June 2006. I hope this had to do with the South Carolina state dance being the shag, and not the term as used by Austin Powers—although that kind of a Shag 'n' Eat would be a hell of a fund-raiser.

Vanilla Ice T

"For state representative, you don't have to tell where you stand on the issues," said Tom Alciere, after being elected to the New Hampshire House of Representatives in November 2000. One of his political issues, Alciere told the *Valley News* of Lebanon, is that he loves it when someone kills a police officer. Here are verbatim excerpts from Alciere's Web site:

> *Too many cops and not enough cop-killers. When soldiers perform the operations of cops, they are, for all intents and purposes, cops. Too many cops turning back relief supply trucks. Not enough cop-killers to get the trucks through.*

Alciere resigned on January 10, 2001, and, if he had any smarts, would have become a lyricist for a gangsta-rap group.

"Tom Alciere is against sodomy laws because having a gay old time doesn't violate anybody's rights."

★ From Tom Alciere's campaign Web site

Suffering Suffragette

"Men should take care of women, and if men were taking care of women, we wouldn't have to vote," said Kansas state senator Kay O'Connor, when asked by the Johnson County League of Women Voters to attend the League's "Celebrate the Right to Vote" luncheon in September 2001. On the subject of the Nineteenth Amendment to the Constitution, which gave women the right to vote, Senator O'Connor was quoted as saying, "The Nineteenth Amendment is around because men weren't doing their jobs, and I think that's sad." The next time Ms. O'Connor decides to run for office, she might consider being a candidate for the "Barefoot and Pregnant" party.

In 2000, Republican Thomas Wesson ran unsuccessfully for constable in the largely Hispanic Sixth Precinct of Dallas, despite changing his name to Tomás Eduardo Wesson.

Daddy Dearest

According to an April 20, 2006, article in the *Arizona Daily Star*, Republican Mike Harris contributed $100,000 of his own money to his gubernatorial campaign and promised to donate $150,000 more. Six months before that, Harris's wife took him to court because he was $22,500 behind in alimony and owed her $44,000 from the sale of their farm—the sale of which he did not disclose. Harris, claiming near bankruptcy, was able to convince a judge to cut his $2,000 monthly child-support payments in half for his seven-year-old son. When asked if he would start paying more than $1,000 in child support after his financial situation had changed, Harris said, "For one kid, for a four-year marriage, it's pretty darn generous." Looks like Hallmark lost another card sale for Father's Day.

Political Portrait

"As you see here, and I think this is maybe the most important prop we'll have during the entire debate, my wife and I have been married forty-seven years. We have twenty kids and grandkids. I'm really proud to say that in the recorded history of our family, we've never had a divorce or any kind of homosexual relationship."

★ Senator James Inhofe (R-OK), gesturing to a prominently displayed family portrait, commenting on the Federal Marriage Amendment, June 6, 2006. I'm sure he meant that no one in his family has had a divorce or any kind of homosexual relationship—but it sure sounded like he was talking about himself and his wife.

Florida state senate candidate Randall Terry, who ran on a family-values campaign, admitted on August 21, 2006, that the family photos in his campaign didn't really contain the whole picture. The photos are missing his two ostracized adopted children: one who is gay and the other who gave birth out of wedlock.

But Who's Counting?

On April 13, 2005, Tom Craddick, the Speaker of the Texas House of Representatives, taught a seventh-grade history class at the Mendez Middle School about our system of government. Craddick proclaimed to the twenty-five or so students that "Up [in Washington, DC] they have 400 and some on the House side—454—and they have fewer on the Senate side—60." Mr. Craddick should get a paddling and be sent to the principal's office, as there are 435 U.S. representatives and 100 U.S. senators.

"We're no longer a superpower. We're a super-duper power."

★ Republican representative Tom "The Hammer" DeLay (R-TX), during an interview with FOX News in 2002, explaining why America must overthrow Saddam Hussein

Doggone It, Doggett

In 2002, Karen Hughes of Austin, Texas, then presidential adviser to George W. Bush, complained openly that Democrat Lloyd Doggett wasn't doing a sufficient job representing her in the U.S. House. Hughes bitterly accused Doggett of bias against her because of her association with the president, and the fact that she is a Republican. Hughes soon realized why Doggett didn't represent her—he wasn't her representative. Her congressman was, in fact, Republican Lamar Smith.

"What we really expect out of the Democrats is for them to treat us as they would liked to have been treated."

★ Then–House minority leader
John Boehner (R-OH), January 4, 2007

It's Good to Be the King

"We must take a strong stand against drugs, and I support strict punishment for individuals involved in the possession or distribution of illegal drugs," wrote Senator Richard Shelby (R-AL) in a letter to the father of a man sentenced to life in prison without parole, even though no drugs, money, or physical evidence were produced, and his accuser later recanted his testimony. Five years later, on July 24, 1998, Senator Shelby's son Claude Shelby was arrested in the Atlanta airport after arriving from London with thirteen grams of hashish in his pocket. He paid a $500 fine on the spot, pled guilty to a misdemeanor possession charge, performed forty hours of community service, and was on probation for one year—but spent not a single hour in jail. The lyrics to the Creedence Clearwater Revival song "Fortunate Son" couldn't be more apropos.

Iraq, You Break

"I was proud the other day when both Republicans and Democrats stood with me in the Rose Garden to announce their support for a clear statement of purpose: You disarm, or we will."

★ George W. Bush, Manchester, New Hampshire, October 5, 2002

"Why do they kill people of other religions because of religion? Why do they hate the Israelis and despise their right to exist? Why do they hate each other? Why do Sunnis kill Shiites? How do they tell the difference? They all look the same to me."

★ Senator Trent Lott (R-MS), September 28, 2006, explaining why he isn't in charge of foreign policy

Nan Nanny Boo-Boo, Stick Your Head in Doo-Doo

During the August 8, 2006, episode of *The Bleepin' Truth* on Tampa, Florida's public-access station, Republican guest Tony Katz threw a chair at county commission candidate Joe Redner, hitting him in the head. Katz had called Redner a liar, and Redner responded by calling Katz "fat boy."

"I think I'd just commit suicide."

Senator John McCain (R-AZ), October 18, 2006, with his possible reaction to the Democrats taking back the Senate in the November 2006 election. (They did—he didn't.)

Being Slaphappy

Following a televised debate on October 22, 2006, Representative Barbara Cubin (R-WY) approached Libertarian candidate Thomas Rankin, who has multiple sclerosis and is confined to a wheelchair, to offer her hand—but not in friendship. "If you weren't sitting in that chair, I'd slap you across the face," Rankin claimed Cubin said. The *Billings Gazette* reported that Cubin "later apologized, saying she may have been influenced by listening to too much Rush Limbaugh." Limbaugh earlier stated that he would slap actor and Parkinson's disease sufferer Michael J. Fox, "if [he'd] just quit bobbing [his] head." Despite the threat, Cubin was reelected to the U.S. House of Representatives—now that's a real slap in the face.

"Katherine Harris is the horse we're going to ride to the finish line, and it's time for us to saddle up."

★ Republican Florida state representative David Rivera, May 2006, on the selection of Katherine Harris as the Republican nominee to run against incumbent Democratic senator Bill Nelson

The Legal Limit

State representative Alan Hale fought furiously to defeat a bill that he thought was "destroying a way of life that has been in Montana for years and years." Hale, who owns a bar in Basin, Montana, complained that tough DUI laws "are destroying small businesses." According to an April 1, 2011, article in the *Billings Gazette*, until 2005, drinking while driving was common and legal outside of towns as long as the driver wasn't drunk. Hale adamantly defended driving while intoxicated by saying that drunks have to get home somehow: "They are not going to hitchhike."

"We have a court that has essentially stuck its finger in God's eye. We have insulted God at the highest levels of our government. Then, we say, 'Why does this happen?' It is happening because God Almighty is lifting His protection from us."

★ Pat Robertson, September 13, 2001,
placing the blame for the 9/11 terrorist attacks
on a liberal Supreme Court

Unfair Usage

"Well, it was an unfair attack on the verbiage that Senator McCain chose to use. The fundamentals that he was having to explain afterwards, he means the workforce, he means ingenuity of the American people. And, of course, that is strong, that is the foundation of our economy. So that was an unfair attack based on verbiage that John McCain used. Certainly, it is a mess, though."

★ Sarah Palin in a September 17, 2008, FOX News interview with Sean Hannity, on why it wasn't fair to use John McCain's own words about the economy against him

Thar She Blows

Texas Republican state representative John Davis of Houston came up with a watertight way of stimulating job growth in Texas: Give a tax break to people who buy yachts valued at more than $250,000. According to an April 24, 2011, article in the *San Antonio Express-News*, Davis declared that a cap on the sales tax on a $250,000 yacht would prompt more people to buy yachts and, therefore, more jobs would be created in Texas.

"The greatest threat to America is not necessarily a recession or even another terrorist attack. The greatest threat to America is a liberal media bias."

★ Representative Lamar Smith (R-TX), June 4, 2009

Taking a
Real Dusting

"I mean, after all, you might remember that some of the initial discussions after September the 11th about potential threat was about crop dusters. Now, they don't have a lot of crop dusters, you know, in Manhattan. They've got a lot of crop dusters in South Carolina, or Texas. In other words, some of the intelligence we were getting was that not only were the enemy willing to use airplanes, obviously, as weapons, but what we were concerned about was that they would use other methods—like using a crop duster to spray a weapons of mass destruction, if possible. It's an indication that we had to be on alert to defend all sites and all locations in our country."

★ George W. Bush, March 27, 2002, in a confusing and grammar-challenged explanation of why we had warnings about crop dusters in the days following 9/11. Warnings such as this one from an October 11, 2001, press conference: "You know, if you find a person that you've never seen before getting in a crop duster that doesn't belong to you, report it."

A Night at the Opera

The High School Symphonic Jazz Choir in Sarah Palin's hometown of Wasilla, Alaska, had been practicing Queen's 1975 rock-opera hit "Bohemian Rhapsody" all year, planning to sing it at graduation. Before the concert, one parent complained that the song was highly inappropriate because its writer, Freddie Mercury, was gay (he died from complications from AIDS in 1991, at forty-five). Principal Dwight Probasco, bending under pressure from a single complaint, pulled the song from the program. The song, however, was included in the program after the ACLU got involved, but Probasco ordered the stanza "Mama / Just killed a man / Put a gun against his head / Pulled my trigger now he's dead" deleted.

"Obama's got a health-care logo that's right out of Adolf Hitler's playbook. . . . Adolf Hitler, like Barack Obama, also ruled by dictate."

★ Rush Limbaugh, *The Rush Limbaugh Show*, August 6, 2009

C-4 for a Quarter

Three aldermen in Dover, New Jersey, became obsessed that their town of eighteen thousand might become a target for terrorism, especially since they were so vulnerable to attack. According to an October 11, 2007, *Star-Ledger* article, the aldermen were convinced that the town's eight hundred gumball machines would be a nefarious way for terrorists to poison their town. They forced one hundred gumball machines that weren't licensed to be dismantled. The chief of police admitted the threat level was overblown: "You'd probably win the lottery first" before falling victim to terrorists' gumballs, he said.

"All of a sudden, we see riots, we see protests, we see people clashing. The next thing we know, there is injured or there is dead people. We don't want to get to that extent."

★ California governor Arnold Schwarzenegger, on the dangers posed if the courts continued to perform same-sex marriages in violation of existing state laws, on NBC'S *Meet the Press*, February 22, 2004

Thomas Jefferson Was a Nazi

"Do you know, where does this phrase 'separation of church and state' come from? It was not in Jefferson's letter to the Danbury Baptists. . . . The exact phrase 'separation of church and state' came out of Adolf Hitler's mouth, that's where it comes from. So the next time your liberal friends talk about the separation of church and state, ask them why they're Nazis."

★ Glen Urquhart, the Tea Party–backed Republican nominee for Delaware's U.S. House of Representatives seat held by Congressman Mike Castle, as reported by the *Hill*, September 17, 2010. (Note: The Danbury letter, written by Thomas Jefferson in 1802, used the phrase "wall of separation between church and state").

"[Republicans] say, 'You're too conservative.' Was Thomas Jefferson too conservative? I'm tired of some people calling me wacky."

Sharron Angle, Nevada GOP Senate nominee and Tea Party favorite, *Las Vegas Review-Journal*, March 21, 2010

Rebel Yell

"It's a part of our history," declared Florida state representative Don Brown. "I appreciate the heritage and the good things that people feel about our past." Brown, a Republican from DeFuniak Springs, Florida, pleaded his case for a bill to commemorate "Confederate Heritage" on state license plates. According to a February 28, 2008, article in the *Walton Sun*, the plates would feature a Confederate battle flag and buttons from a Rebel uniform. In 2009, the Florida Division of the Sons of Confederate Veterans filed a lawsuit against the state of Florida when it refused to print the plates, and won the case.

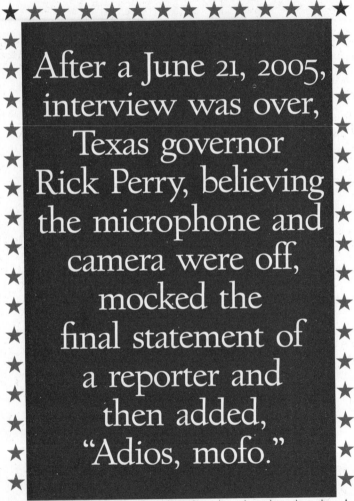

After a June 21, 2005, interview was over, Texas governor Rick Perry, believing the microphone and camera were off, mocked the final statement of a reporter and then added, "Adios, mofo."

Smut Dealers

In order to crack down on the pornography business—or perhaps just to make money from it—Indiana passed a law requiring the sellers of "adult" materials to pay a $250 registration fee with the state. But the law is so loosely written that it includes any book with sexual content, and therefore doesn't exempt traditional bookstores. "This lumps us in with businesses that sell things that you can't even mention in a family newspaper," complained the owner of Fine Print Book Store in Greencastle. "The way we read this bill, if you stock a single book with sexual content—even a novel or a book about sex education—you will have to register as a business that sells sexually explicit material," said Chris Finan, president of the American Booksellers Foundation for Free Expression. According to a March 26, 2008, Associated Press article, Indiana state senator Brent Steele, who cosponsored the law, said, "We believe [this law] is a violation of the First Amendment." But, he continued, "I just don't think that their concern is legitimate."

Animal Husbandry

"If you're oriented toward animals, bestiality, then, you know, that's not something that can be used, held against you or any bias be held against you for that. Which means you'd have to strike any laws against bestiality; if you're oriented toward corpses, toward children, you know, there are all kinds of perversions . . . pedophiles or necrophiliacs or what most would say is perverse sexual orientations."

★ Representative Louie Gohmert (R-TX), October 6, 2009, arguing on the House floor that a hate-crimes bill passed by Congress would lead to the legalization of bestiality, pedophilia, and necrophilia

"If I see someone come in that's got a diaper on his head and a fan belt wrapped around the diaper on his head, that guy needs to be pulled over."

★ Representative John Cooksey (R-LA), during a post-9/11 radio interview, as reported by the *Washington Post*, September 20, 2001

Ah, Nuts

Carey Baker, the Florida Senate's transportation chairman, spent two days insisting his committee continue debating his amendment to the state's transportation bill. "There's got to be better things for us to be spending our time debating," said an exhausted Steve Geller, Florida Senate minority leader. Baker's provision would levy a sixty-dollar fine for anyone installing Truck Nutz on their vehicles. "Truck Nutz," in case you don't know, are dangling items that "resemble reproductive glands." According to a May 9, 2008, article in the *Orlando Sentinel*, the senate's two-day fight was in vain, as the house refused the bill and it shriveled up and died. The newspaper, however, said the senate needed to sack up and focus on real issues, because "State finances are a disaster—funding for education was cut, commuter rail was dumped and help for disabled people was slashed."

> "I don't believe there's any issue that's more important than this one."

Senator David Vitter (R-LA), June 7, 2006, discussing not the war in Iraq, the national debt, or our inferior schools—but the ultimately failed constitutional amendment banning same-sex marriage

The Politics of Deception

The reelection campaign of Mayor Becky Miller of Carrollton, Texas, had a comfortable nine-point lead going into the election until the *Dallas Morning News* pointed out some questionable biographical bullet points in an article on May 7, 2008. Miller claimed her brother was killed in the Vietnam War, but her father was quoted as saying that her only brother was alive and was never in the military. (Miller claimed her father had Alzheimer's.) Miller finally gave the paper her brother's name, and reporters discovered that the soldier in question was black, which Miller is not. She also stated in her biography that she was once engaged to the Eagles' Don Henley, and was a backup singer for Linda Ronstadt and Jackson Browne—and the reason no one remembers her is because she used to go by the name "Pinky." Miller was voted out of office—and that's the truth.

In 2004, the U.S. Department of Agriculture concluded that "batter-coated French fries are a fresh vegetable." And since the Reagan administration classified ketchup as a vegetable in 1981, kids are finally eating healthy.

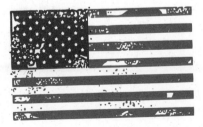

I Can Make 'Em and I Can Break 'Em

Reporter: "The FISA law was implemented in 1978 in part because of revelations that the National Security Agency was spying domestically. What is wrong with that law if you feel you have to circumvent it and, as you just admitted, expand presidential power?"

George W. Bush: "May I—if I might, you said that I have to circumvent it. There—wait a minute. That's a—there's something—it's like saying, you know, you're breaking the law. I'm not. See, that's what you've got to understand. I am upholding my duty, and at the same time, doing so under the law and with the Constitution behind me. That's just very important for you to understand. Secondly, the FISA law was written in 1978. We're having this discussion in 2006. It's a different world. And FISA is still an important tool. It's an important

tool. And we still use that tool. But also—and we—
look—I said, look, is it possible to conduct this
program under the old law? And people said, it
doesn't work in order to be able to do the job we
expect us to do."

★ George W. Bush, January 26, 2006, taking the
advice of "people" to ignore the Foreign Intelligence
Surveillance Act because it was written in 1978 and
gets in the way of the "job we expect us to do"

Hunter Hunt

Republican U.S. representative Duncan Hunter of California had what he thought was a great idea to help feed the refugees who have fled Darfur for Chad, and he contacted the U.S. embassy in N'Djamena. Hunter offered to help distribute food at a camp and then lead a hunting party for wildebeest to feed the 230,000 refugees. The U.S. State Department appreciated Hunter's concern, and replied that he would be welcome to come and observe the delivery of the already abundant emergency supply of food. But as for his second proposal, "Regarding the Congressman's desire to hunt wildebeest and distribute the cured meat to refugees, wildebeest are not present in Chad." Even if there were, "The Government of Chad does not permit the hunting of large mammals." According to a July 23, 2008, article in the *Washington Post*, after receiving the embassy's reply, Hunter canceled his visit.

"We finally cleaned up public housing in New Orleans. We couldn't do it, but God did."

★ Representative Richard Baker (R-LA) to lobbyists, after Hurricane Katrina, as quoted in the *Wall Street Journal*, September 9, 2005

Grabbing the Bull by the Horns

Every year, *Texas Monthly* publishes its Bum Steer Awards, a review of the strange, stupid, and embarrassing antics in Texas. In its year 2000 issue, the magazine reported that the U.S. Fish and Wildlife Service wanted further research into the environmental impact of a proposed road and bridge below the Lake Georgetown dam on endangered cave bugs. It quoted Williamson County commissioner Greg Boatright as saying, "You know the best way you can do research is to pour about fifty gallons of gas down there and light a match so you can see."

Texas governor Rick Perry told the audience he was glad to be in Abilene to start his 2006 reelection campaign. He was in Midland at the time.

The Dating Game

Question: "Are you offended by the phrase 'Under God' in the Pledge of Allegiance? Why or why not?"

Sarah Palin: "Not on your life. If it was good enough for the founding fathers, it's good enough for me, and I'll fight in defense of our Pledge of Allegiance."

★ 2006 questionnaire for Alaska's gubernatorial race.
The pledge was written in 1892, and the words
"under God" were not added until June 14, 1954.

"Gay marriage should be between a man and a woman."

★ California governor Arnold Schwarzenegger, in a radio interview with Sean Hannity, as reported by the *New York Daily News*, August 29, 2003

Give a Hoot

Missouri Republican state senator Kevin Engler had wanted to crack down on littering for six years without success, and finally proposed cracking the necks of people who litter. "I think killing one or two of them would be a fine first start, and then the rest would fall in line," Engler said on the senate floor after introducing a bill calling for the death penalty for littering. According to a February 12, 2009, article in the *Park Hills Daily Journal*, Engler said, "When they're [littering] with their kids in the backseat, they're teaching them to be white trash and I'm sick of it. These dumb rednecks I've got in my district throw it in the back of their truck expecting it not to blow out and then they just drive down the road." When criticized for calling his constituents "rednecks" and "white trash," Engler said, "The only people I called names are the ones doing it. If they are offended, good."

"Canadian Prime Minister Doesn't Think Bush Is 'a Moron'"

★ Reuters headline, November 21, 2002

According to His Plan

"God is giving a plan I think to me that is not really a plan. . . . The problem is that I think the plan that the Lord would have us follow is hard for people to understand. . . . Because of my track record with you who have been here for a long time—because of my track record with you, I beg of you to help me get this message out, and I beg of you to pray for clarity on my part."

★ Glenn Beck, *The Glenn Beck Program*, April 20, 2010

"If I were to lose my mind right now and pick one of you up and bash your head against the floor and kill you, would that be right?"

★ Presidential candidate Alan Keyes, enlightening a class of fifth-graders on January 31, 2000, about the morality of abortion

John, I Am
Your Father

"I'm telling you, they're shooting at me from everywhere. Everybody's against me. Governor Engler, Governor Bush, all the governors, all the senators, but we're going to kill them, right? We're going to get them. I'm getting out of that Death Star, and we're going to win this election."

★ Senator John McCain, February 22, 2000, rallying his troops, or maybe his clone troopers or imperial stormtroopers, in Michigan during his failed 2000 presidential bid

"I feel like Luke Skywalker trying to get out of the Death Star."

★ Presidential candidate and possible space cadet John McCain describing his intergalactic battle with his own party concerning campaign finance reform on February 5, 2000

Hi, Ho, Hi, Ho, It's Off to War We Go

Brian Williams: "Do you believe this war was an elective on your part? Or did this have to come out of 9/11?"

George W. Bush: "Hmm, interesting question. Well, first of all, troops don't move unless I give the order. So, from that sense it was elective. I mean, I could have said, no, we'll try to, you know, hope for the best with Saddam Hussein. Remember, at the time, we didn't know the facts on the ground. We—everybody thought the guy had weapons of mass destruction. Everybody knew that he'd used weapons of mass destruction and had provided safe haven for terrorists. I mean, those were facts. Whether or not it had to happen is—it didn't have to happen since a human being made the decision. Whether or not it needed to happen, I'm still convinced it needed to happen."

★ *NBC Nightly News with Brian Williams,*
December 12, 2005

A Political Black Eye

During the reelection campaign of Republican U.S. representative Don Sherwood of Pennsylvania, his mistress not only confessed to their twenty-nine-year affair but also accused him of beating and strangling her. Sherwood decided to run television ads to fight the negative impact of his affair and possible abuse. "While I'm truly sorry for disappointing you," said Sherwood in a commercial, "I never wavered from my commitment to reduce taxes, create jobs, and bring home our fair share." The ad continued with "Should you forgive me, you can count on me to keep on fighting hard for you and your family." I don't know if the word "fighting" was the best choice for an accused abuser. But Sherwood couldn't put the stranglehold on the election, and lost to Democrat Chris Carney. I'm sure Sherwood was all choked up.

"I favor the death penalty for abortionists and other people who take life."

★ Senate candidate Tom Coburn, in a July 10, 2004, interview with The Associated Press. He admitted to performing two abortions himself as a doctor (to save the lives of mothers with congenital heart disease), but he opposes the procedure in cases of rape.

Off to the Races

"[Alaska's founders'] remarkably succinct words guided us in all of our efforts in serving you and putting you first, and we have done our best to fulfill promises that I made on Alaska Day, 2005, when I first asked for the honor of serving you."

★ **Governor Sarah Palin, July 26, 2009,**
resigning with a year and a half left in her term

"The Antichrist is probably a Jew alive in Israel today."

★ Pat Robertson, "The Christian Paradox," *Harper's Magazine*, August 2005

Going Off
Half-Cocked

Harold Gunn of Houston, Texas, lost his race for state representative in the 2000 Republican primary after it was revealed that in 1983 he not only wrote but also appeared in a nudie flick entitled *The Great Texas Show*. Among other scenes, the film featured a naked woman jogging and another woman slathering herself with motor oil.

"These are beautiful properties with basketball courts, bathroom facilities, toilet facilities. Many young people would love to get the hell out of cities."

Carl Paladino, Tea Party-backed candidate for governor of New York, describing his idea to transform prisons into dorms for welfare recipients to The Associated Press on August 23, 2010

I Have a Bone to Pick with You

At a congressional hearing in February 1994, Mollie Beattie, then director of the U.S. Fish and Wildlife Service, argued with Alaska representative Don Young about exempting Alaska natives from laws protecting ocean animals. Beattie expressed her concern that seals, polar bears, and certain other animals were being slaughtered solely for their gall bladders and reproductive organs, which in some Asian countries are considered delicacies or aphrodisiacs. Young's tempered flared, and he grabbed a prop he had brought along and started slamming it into his hand as he spoke with Beattie. The prop was an eighteen-inch-long walrus penis.

"That is not within the scope of the powers that are given to the federal government."

★ Joe Miller, Alaska GOP Senate candidate, arguing in an October 7, 2010, ABC News interview that the federal minimum wage, which was established when Congress passed the Fair Labor Standards Act in 1938, was unconstitutional, and should be left to the states to decide

At Least There Was an Entrance Strategy

Brian Williams: "A lot of people have seen in this series of speeches you're giving on Iraq a movement in your position. They call it an acknowledgment that perhaps the mission has not gone as it was originally planned—three points: that the U.S. would be welcomed as liberators, that General Shinseki, when he said this would take hundreds of thousands of troops in his farewell speech, might have been right. And third, that it wasn't a self-sustaining war in terms of the oil revenue. Do you concede those three points might not have gone as planned?"

George W. Bush: "Review them with me again."

Williams: "Number one—that we'd be welcomed as liberators?"

Bush: "I think we are welcomed. But it was not a peaceful welcome."

★ *NBC Nightly News with Brian Williams,*
December 12, 2005

Foster a Resentment

In August 2000, Pat Buchanan's Reform Party running mate for the 2000 presidential election, Ezola Foster, a longtime opponent of most government social programs, admitted that she had submitted a false document in 1996 in order to get California worker-compensation benefits. Foster claimed to have had a "mental illness" that entitled her to draw money for a year before her retirement as a typing teacher in 1997. When the issue of her mental stability came up during the campaign, Foster claimed her "mental illness" was worked out "between my doctor and my attorney. It's whatever the doctor said that, after working with my attorney, was best to help me." Foster founded Black Americans for Family Values, and is the author of the book *What's Right for All Americans*.

Whatever Gets You Through the Night

"The homosexual marriage lobby, as well as the polygamist lobby, they share the same goal of essentially breaking down all state-regulated marriage requirements to just one, and that one is consent. In doing so, they're paving the way for illegal protection of such practices as homosexual marriage, unrestricted sexual conduct between adults and children, group marriage, incest, and, you know, if it feels good, do it."

★ Senator James Inhofe (R-OK), remarking on the Senate floor about the Federal Marriage Amendment, June 6, 2006

"You're dealing with people who are professional race-baiters, who make a very good living off this kind of thing. They make more money off of race than any slave trader ever. It's time groups like the NAACP went to the trash heap of history where they belong, with all the other vile racist groups that emerged in our history."

★ Mark Williams, national spokesman for the Tea Party Express, NPR, July 14, 2010

And Never a Train Shall Meet

In the 2007 federal budget, $4 million was added by then–Senate Appropriations Committee chairman Ted Stevens (R-AK) for the Northern Line Extension. The new railroad line extension would provide a direct route from North Pole, Alaska (pop. 1,597), to Delta Junction, Alaska (pop. 812), which are only eighty-two miles apart. When Congress spends our tax dollars on useless pork projects like this, we ought to run them out of town on a rail.

"The Girl Scouts allow homosexuals and atheists to join their ranks, and they have become a pro-abortion, feminist training corps. If the Girl Scouts of America can't get back to teaching real character, perhaps it will be time to look for our cookies elsewhere."

★ Posted and then removed from the Web site of Hans Zeiger, 2010 Republican candidate for Congress in Washington State, as reported by the *News Tribune*, September 4, 2010

Shooting His Mouth Off

"What Mr. Loughner knows is that he has the full support of a major political party in this country. . . . He knows that. . . . The Democrat party is attempting to find anybody but him to blame. He knows if he plays his cards right, he's just a victim. . . . This guy clearly understands he's getting all the attention, and he understands he's got a political party doing everything it can, plus a local sheriff doing everything that they can, to make sure he's not convicted of murder—but something lesser."

★ Rush Limbaugh, *The Rush Limbaugh Show*, January 11, 2011, on Arizona shooter Jared Lee Loughner, who is charged with the January 8, 2011, Tucson, Arizona, shooting that killed six people, including nine-year-old Christina-Taylor Green and U.S. federal judge John Roll, and injured fourteen others, including U.S. representative Gabrielle Giffords

"Ground Zero Mosque supporters: Doesn't it stab you in the heart, as it does ours throughout the heartland? Peaceful Muslims, pls refudiate."

Sarah Palin, in a July 18, 2010, tweet that she quickly removed after being ridiculed for inventing the word "refudiate"

Going Away Present

In November 2006, as Arkansas governor Mike Huckabee was preparing to leave office, he took the time to set up a wedding registry at two department stores, which might lead one to believe that Huckabee was getting married. But at that time, Huckabee had been happily married to Janet Huckabee for thirty-two years—so why did he set up two registries? Was he having an affair? Nope. Arkansas law prohibits gifts to public officials of more than $100, with a few exceptions—wedding gifts being one of them. I wouldn't be surprised if Huckabee set up a registry for a baby shower next.

"They are also building schools for the Afghan children so that there is hope and opportunity in our neighboring country of Afghanistan."

★ Sarah Palin, during an October 5, 2008, fund-raising speech in San Francisco. She can apparently see Afghanistan from her front porch, too.

And the Buggy You Road in On!

"I'm telling you that this works. You know, before we all started having health care, in the olden days, our grandparents, they would bring a chicken to the doctor. They would say, 'I'll paint your house.' I mean, that's the old days of what people would do to get health care with your doctors. Doctors are very sympathetic people. I'm not backing down from that system."

★ Sue Lowden, 2010 Republican Senate candidate in Nevada, *Nevada NewsMakers*, April 19, 2010, articulating her vision of how the American health-care system should revert back to the days of bartering

"American scientific companies are cross-breeding humans and animals and coming up with mice with fully functioning human brains."

Christine O'Donnell, *The O'Reilly Factor*, November 15, 2007, discussing cloning

It's Who You Know

In August 2001, Montana governor Judy Martz
answered her door and found a member of her staff,
chief policy adviser Shane Hedges, covered in blood
and in a state of panic. He told her he had been
involved in a single-car accident and that the passenger
in his car, Montana house majority leader Paul Sliter,
had died. Martz took pity on the frightened young
man and did what anyone would do in that situation—
she washed his clothes. The police who had been
collecting evidence from the accident scene didn't learn
about the laundered clothes until months later. Hedges
was sentenced to community service and six months
in a halfway house for negligent homicide and driving
while drunk. But I'm sure with good friends like
Governor Martz, Hedges's record, like his clothes, will
be wiped clean.

Don't Let Him See a Child Psychiatrist, Either

"Regardless of the fact of whether I'm guilty or unguilty, there are no children at the county legislature," said Richard Hobbs, who ultimately lost his campaign for the Westchester County, New York, legislature as a candidate in the Right to Life Party. Hobbs was explaining to a reporter in November 2001 why being a twice-convicted pedophile wasn't relevant to his campaign.

Hobbs, who is also a professional clown, was back in the news a few years later when a judge ordered Westchester County to pay him $2,500 for violating his rights after refusing to allow him to perform his clown act in front of children at a local amusement park.

Do What I Say, Not What I Do

"Spam is an annoying, intrusive form of e-mail that almost all of us receive but few of us want," said Florida attorney general Charlie Crist. So when he decided to run for governor, he touted his crusade against spammers and how he helped stiffen the law against unsolicited e-mail. Then, in order to garner support for his candidacy, Crist began sending out campaign e-mails on December 21, 2005, based in part on addresses obtained from the state's Web site. Crist's political director Arlene DiBenigno defended her boss by claiming, "It's not spam. It's political speech." So the Monty Python skit could go "Spam, spam, spam, spam, spam, spam, baked beans, spam, spam, spam, and political speech."

"An Indonesian Muslim turned welfare thug and racist in chief."

Mark Williams, national spokesman for the Tea Party Express, speaking about Barack Obama, on his blog on September 14, 2009

The Check's in the Mail

Jose A. Riesco, campaign spokesman for U.S. representative Lincoln Diaz-Balart (R-FL), decided pleading incompetence was the best way out of a sticky situation. On December 20, 2000, Riesco told the *Miami Daily Business Review* that forty-five illegal campaign checks, totalling nearly $30,000, were returned as Representative Diaz-Balart promised, and as required by law, immediately after they were discovered. But, strangely, none of the forty-five checks were cashed until eight months later, giving Diaz-Balart full use of the illegal campaign contributions through the end of the election. Why did it take so long for the checks to be received and cashed? Somehow every single one of the forty-five checks was lost in the mail—"poorly addressed, things like that," Riesco said. Diaz-Balart was reelected to another congressional term, and with the horrible postal service, he was lucky he wasn't dependent upon absentee ballots.

Hobby Lobby

Representative Nancy Argenziano was upset that a nursing-home protection bill for which she had fought had been significantly altered thanks to the help of a notoriously antagonistic industry lobbyist. Argenziano wanted to express her anger for the Associated Industries of Florida's lobbyist, and decided to send her a pie—a cow pie. So on May 2, 2001, Argenziano lovingly gift wrapped and shipped a twenty-five-pound box of cow manure to the lobbyist. No matter what people thought about Argenziano's gift, the one thing they can't say is that she didn't give a shit.

"My number-one goal is to not go to jail."

★ Congresswoman-elect Michele Bachmann (R-MN), during "freshman orientation" for new members of Congress, November 13, 2006

Barack Attack

"I am not saying that Barack Obama is a fascist. If I'm not mistaken, in the early days of Adolf Hitler, they were very happy to line up for help there, as well. I mean, the companies were like, 'Hey, wait a minute. We can get, you know, we can get out of trouble here. They can help, et cetera, et cetera.'"

★ Glenn Beck, *The Glenn Beck Program*, April 1, 2009, comparing government bailouts of auto companies to the actions of German companies during the rise of Hitler

President George W. Bush's education secretary Margaret Spellings was beaten on *Celebrity Jeopardy!* in November 2006 by Michael McKean, best known for his role as "Lenny" on the television show *Laverne and Shirley* and for the movie *This Is Spinal Tap*.

Macaca, You Caca

At a campaign rally in southwest Virginia on August 11, 2006, Senator George Allen (R-VA) told the crowd he was "going to run this campaign on positive, constructive ideas." He then pointed at S. R. Sidarth, a twenty-year-old Virginian native of Indian descent, saying, "This fellow here, over here with the yellow shirt, Macaca, or whatever his name is. He's with my opponent. . . . Let's give a welcome to Macaca, here." Allen said he didn't know what the word "Macaca" meant, but thought it sounded like "Mohawk," which he claimed his staff called Sidarth because of his haircut (Sidarth wore a mullet, not a Mohawk). The word "Macaca," depending on how you spell it, is either a monkey indigenous to Asia, a town in South Africa, or a racial slur against African immigrants. Allen apologized the following week.

Standing Room Only

Democratic state representative Chuck Graham of Missouri was speaking to the legislative body during an orientation session in December 2002 when freshman representative Cynthia Davis interrupted him on a point of order. Davis recited that the state's parliamentary procedure required members to be standing in order to speak, and Graham, who was sitting, therefore, was out of order. Despite Davis's reprimand, Graham remained in his chair. Was he being defiant? No. Graham, a representative since 1996, was paralyzed and had been confined to a wheelchair after a devastating car accident twenty-one years earlier. Graham may be paralyzed, but it was Davis who wound up looking lame.

"That's right, I said I'm a hooker. I have to go up to total strangers, ask them for money, and get them to expect me to be there when they need me. What does that sound like to you?"

★ Representative Ginny Brown-Waite (R-FL), explaining her job description at the Women Impacting Public Policy conference, as reported by the *Hill*, October 4, 2005

Our Turn
in the Barrel

When Representative Don Young (R-AK) was asked
by reporters on September 19, 2005, why he didn't
divert funds from his infamous "Bridge to Nowhere"
and use the money to help ease the suffering in New
Orleans after Hurricane Katrina, he yelled back, "They
can kiss my ear! That is the dumbest thing I've ever
heard." The "Bridge to Nowhere" (which has yet to be
built but has cost taxpayers $223 million already) will
be larger than the Brooklyn Bridge, and almost as long
as the Golden Gate, and will connect a town with
8,900 people to a town with 50 people. When told
by a *New York Times* reporter that another congressman
had outspent him in pork projects, Young replied,
"I'd like to be a little oinker, myself. If he's the chief
porker, I'm upset." He's the one who called himself a
pig—not me.

Representative Young has also earmarked $200 million for another
"bridge to nowhere," which will connect Anchorage to a town
with one tenant and a handful of houses.

Dress for Success

A memo from the members of the South Carolina legislature's "Men's Caucus" surfaced in 2001 that advised female pages to wear skimpy clothes and short skirts and optional underwear. All 124 members were requested to attend a two-hour seminar on gender, racial, and ethnic sensitivity, scheduled at the start of the 2002 session. Many of the house members turned a cold shoulder to the sensitivity training, including Republican John Graham Altman from Charleston, who said, "I won't be able to attend. I forgot to pack a dress." Altman is not only insensitive—he's also insensible.

"The public doesn't care about facts and figures."

★ California gubernatorial candidate Arnold Schwarzenegger, August 20, 2003, to a gathering of several hundred reporters after the inaugural meeting of his "Economic Recovery Council"

I Apologize for My Apology

"I'm ashamed of what happened in the White House yesterday. I think it is a tragedy in the first proportion that a private corporation can be subjected to what I would characterize as a shakedown—in this case a $20 billion shakedown. . . . I'm only speaking for myself. I'm not speaking for anyone else, but I apologize. I do not want to live in a country where anytime a citizen or a corporation does something that is legitimately wrong, [it is] subject to some sort of political pressure that, again, in my words, amounts to a shakedown. So, I apologize."

★ Representative Joe Barton (R-TX), during a June 17, 2010, House Committee on Energy and Commerce hearing with BP CEO Tony Hayward, who himself was apologizing for his company's massive oil spill in the Gulf of Mexico. President Obama pressured BP to set up a $20 billion fund for damages to pay for the gulf oil spill. The next day, Barton, the biggest recipient of oil- and gas-industry campaign contributions in the House of Representatives, was forced by Republican leaders to apologize for his BP apology.

The Dark Side of Politics

On April 7, 2003, Representative Barbara Cubin (R-WY), debating a gun-control bill on the House floor, commented, "My sons are twenty-five and thirty. They are blond haired and blue eyed. One amendment today said we could not sell guns to anybody under drug treatment. So does that mean if you go into a black community, you cannot sell a gun to any black person?" Representative Melvin Watt (D-NC), who is black, interrupted Cubin and demanded she retract the statement. Cubin claimed she did not mean to offend her "neighbors" on the Democratic side, and that her comment was within House rules.

"Sometimes, based on the votes that get cast, you wonder whether they're more interested in the rights of the terrorists than in protecting the American people."

★ House majority leader John Boehner (R-OH),
September 12, 2006,
on the Democrats in Congress

Close Encounters
of the
Legislative Kind

Representative Dan Foley proposed legislation on March 10, 2003, to create a special day to honor aliens. I'm not talking about illegal aliens or legal aliens or even human aliens—I mean aliens that are out of this world. Foley said he would like "Extraterrestrial Culture Day" to commemorate "the many visitations, sightings, unexplained mysteries, and technological advances . . . of alien beings." Foley's district is Roswell, New Mexico, the site where some say aliens crash-landed in 1947, and his legislation would "enhance relationships among all the citizens of the cosmos, known and unknown." Foley was so excited he had to "phone home" after his proposal won approval in the House.

"**God is the one who chooses our rulers.**"

★ Representative Katherine Harris (R-FL), explaining why the separation of church and state is "a lie," *Florida Baptist Witness*, August 24, 2006

A Shocking Proposal

While a New Mexico representative is building a bridge to reach out to aliens (see page 189) a representative from Iowa is proposing to build a wall of separation. "I also say we need to do a few other things on top of that wall, and one of them being to put a little bit of wire on top here to provide a disincentive for people to climb over the top or put a ladder there. We could also electrify this wire with the kind of current that would not kill somebody, but it would simply be a discouragement for them to be fooling around with it. We do that with livestock all the time."

★ Representative Steve King (R-IA), July 11, 2006, showing a scale model of a twelve-foot concrete wall topped with an electrified fence he proposes to run two thousand miles along the border of the United States and Mexico

"Isn't that the ultimate homeland security, standing up and defending marriage?"

Senator Rick Santorum (R-PA), on the Senate floor, regarding the failed constitutional amendment banning gay marriage, July 14, 2004

Al Gore-ing

"Al Gore's not going to be rounding up Jews and exterminating them. It is the same tactic, however. The goal is different. The goal is globalization. The goal is global carbon tax. . . . You need to have fear. You needed to have the fear of starvation. You needed to have the fear of the whole place going to hell in a handbasket. Which—do we have that fear now with global warming? . . . Then you have to discredit the scientists that say 'That's not right.' And you must silence all dissenting voices. That's what Hitler did. That's what Al Gore, the U.N., and everybody on the global-warming bandwagon [are doing]."

★ Glenn Beck, *The Glenn Beck Program*, April 30, 2007, likening Al Gore's film *An Inconvenient Truth* with the Nazi extermination of the Jews

The Real Pork Barrel

The day after the South Carolina House of Representatives overrode 105 out of 106 budget vetoes by Governor Mark Sanford, he visited the state house with a couple of pigs. By "pigs" I don't mean police officers; I mean real pigs or, in this case, two piglets—one named "Pork" and the other named "Barrel." "There was a lot of pork eating yesterday [May 26, 2004]," said Sanford, juggling the squirming pigs. But not everyone was squealing with delight at the governor's ham-handed approach. "This is the people's house," said House Speaker David Wilkins. "I think he defiled it in order to get TV coverage." But what really got defiled was the governor when the two little piggies went wee-wee-wee (and poop-poop-poop) all over his suit and shoes.

The Ninety-One-Year-Old Virgin

"What occurred to me that morning is something that I imagine a lot of you have thought about, and he's probably figured it out by now. There probably are not seventy-two virgins in the hell he's at, and if there are, they probably all look like Helen Thomas."

★ Representative Steve King (R-IA), June 17, 2006, at the Iowa State Republican Convention discussing the death of terrorist leader Abu Musab al-Zarqawi. (Helen Thomas, who is ninety-one, was a veteran White House correspondent until 2010.)

"It is a better and more important story than losing a couple of soldiers every day."

★ Representative George Nethercutt (R-WA), speaking to a group of sixty-five at an October 13, 2003, meeting at the University of Washington's Evans School of Public Affairs, explaining how the rebuilding of Iraq was a better news story than American soldiers killed in battle

Putting His Finger in the Dyke

In the February 23, 2005, edition of the *American Prospect*, Senator Tom Coburn (R-OK) claimed the small town of Coalgate, Oklahoma, was overrun with inhabitants from the Isle of Lesbos. "Lesbianism is so rampant in some of the schools in southeast Oklahoma that they'll only let one girl go to the bathroom." I'm sure Coburn meant they only let one girl go to the bathroom at a time, otherwise there would be a whole different type of crisis. However, according to the most recent figures, there are only 234 students at Coalgate High School, and less than half of them are girls. So it's doubtful that much of anything can really be said to be "rampant." The only thing that I see that's rampant is Coburn's fantasy about lesbians in the bathroom.

"Some of us believe they would be better off in orphanages than to be raised in the homosexual, bisexual, because that's a learned behavior."

★ Texas Republican state representative
Robert Talton, April 2005

Sauron Santorum

To show that he's got a solid and realistic grasp on the situation in Iraq, Senator Rick Santorum (R-PA) told a reporter from the *Bucks County Courier Times* on October 17, 2006, "As the hobbits are going up Mount Doom, the Eye of Mordor is being drawn somewhere else." (The Eye of Mordor was how the evil Lord Sauron searched for the Ring that would consolidate his power over Middle-earth in *The Lord of the Rings*.) "It's being drawn to Iraq, and it's not being drawn to the U.S. You know what? I want to keep it on Iraq. I don't want the Eye to come back here to the United States." I'll bet Santorum now wishes he had said "precious" little.

"How many Palestinians were on those airplanes on September 9th? None."

★ Former vice president Dan Quayle, MSNBC, April 30, 2002

A Family Affair

"I think incest can be handled as a family matter within the family. The people know about it, and they can get more serious about it. But I don't think it's rape because of the awareness of it within the family."

★ Republican Jay Dickey, candidate for U.S. Congress, at an El Dorado, Arkansas, Rotary Club in July 1992, explaining why he's against the incest exception many right-to-lifers make for abortion

Representative John Boozman (R-AR) allowed his domain name, boozmanforcongress.com, to lapse, so for a while visitors trying to find information about Boozman found themselves at a gay-porn site featuring "the hottest studs on the Internet."

Damage Control

During a trial in November 2001, Pennsylvania state representative Jane Baker told a jury she "needs help with reading and understanding material and carrying on conversations" after suffering head injuries in a traffic accident. Baker said her cognitive abilities had been so damaged that she was "virtually unemployable"—except for her position in the legislature. She promised, however, that in spite of her brain trauma she would run for a second term in 2002. According to the *Allentown Morning Call*, the jury awarded her $2.9 million. I hope they thought of it as a bribe not to run.

Joseph Oliverio, while running for governor of West Virginia, admitted in February 2000 that he'd had sixty speeding tickets and been arrested more than 150 times for fighting.

Science Shmience

"As a matter of fact, carbon dioxide is portrayed as harmful! But there isn't even one study that can be produced that shows carbon dioxide is a harmful gas. There isn't one such study because carbon dioxide is not a harmful gas—it is a harmless gas. Carbon dioxide is natural. It is not harmful. It is part of Earth's life cycle."

★ Representative Michelle Bachmann (R-MN),
on the House floor, Earth Day, April 22, 2009

"To be very blunt, and God watch over Paul's soul, I am a 99 percent improvement over Paul Wellstone. Just about on every issue."

★ Senator Norm Coleman (R-MN), as quoted in *Roll Call*, April 7, 2003, positioning himself against Paul Wellstone, the former Democratic senator from Minnesota who died in a plane crash on October 25, 2002.

Mr. Robinson's Neighborhood

According to Vernon Robinson (R-NC), same-sex marriage will lead to "civil unions for three men, then four or five, then two transvestites, a pedophile, a lesbian, and a partridge in a pear tree." Vernon, an African-American, is legendary for his reverse-racist remarks, his outspokenness, and his offbeat ads, such as the one in which he announced "Jesse Helms is back! And this time he's black." One of Robinson's ads reminded listeners about the difficulties liberals have in admitting that "black mothers need to stop having eight babies by seven different fathers, stop talking street-talk jive like 'Yo, dawg, peep my bling-bling.'" If Robinson were white, he would be labeled a racist—but since he's black, he should be labeled . . . uh, a racist.

During a June
debate in 2002
between Republican
candidates for
Alabama secretary of
state, Dave Thomas
angrily challenged
opponent Dean Young
to a fistfight.

Historical Mistake

"This was a war of Obama's choosing. This is not something the United States has actively prosecuted or wanted to engage in."

★ Michael Steele, Republican National Committee chairman, at a July 2, 2010, Connecticut fund-raiser, completely rewriting history about the war in Afghanistan, which President Bush launched following the 9/11 terrorist attacks

"It's the most difficult [decision] I've made in my entire life, except the one I made in 1978 when I decided to get a bikini wax."

— Arnold Schwarzenegger, August 6, 2003, announcing his candidacy for California governor on *The Tonight Show with Jay Leno*

The Lighter Side of the Dark Side

In an article in the November 17, 2003, *Dartmouth Review*, the reporter asked presidential candidate Robert Haines about the moral issues facing the nation and our churches, to which he replied, "Well, the infiltration of the Church's body by the Dark Side, OK? This is not by coincidence that all these things are happening. This is a deliberate attempt by the Dark Side to infiltrate the church. . . . People working for Satan himself. Yes, the Dark Side, they are working for Satan. These people are not worshipping God, the most High, the most Almighty, or Jesus Christ. They are doing the work of the Devil—Satan himself." It always amazes me why people like this don't get elected more often.

"We thank God for those young people that do it every day and every night—to fight this enemy that's a taxi cab driver in the daytime, but a killer at night."

★ Senator Conrad Burns (R-MT),
The Associated Press, September 1, 2006

The Ignorant Masses

To show his respect and gratitude for the citizens who voted him into office in November 2000, New Hampshire Republican state representative Tom Alciere went online on January 3, 2001, and posted that he'd been elected by a "bunch of fat, stupid, ugly old ladies that watch soap operas, play bingo, read tabloids and don't know the metric system." You'll be glad to know that in the September 12, 2006, primary for state senator, those same voters overwhelmingly elected Dennis Hogan in a write-in campaign, beating Alciere by an 8–1 margin. Now Alciere has plenty of time to watch soap operas, play bingo, read tabloids, and learn the metric system himself.

Representative Lee Terry (R-NE) accidentally gave out the wrong 800 number to constituents looking for updates on the Medicare bill. The erroneous number connected callers to a sex chat line seductively answered with "Welcome to Intimate Connections."

Representative De Sade

"Now I've seen what happened in Abu Ghraib, and Abu Ghraib was not torture. It was outrageous, outrageous involvement of National Guard troops from [Maryland] who were involved in a sex ring, and they took pictures of soldiers who were naked. And they did other things that were just outrageous. But it wasn't torture."

★ Representative Christopher Shays (R-CT), in an October 11, 2006, debate with Democratic challenger Diane Farrell. Shays obviously realized the true value of having a woman lead you around naked on a dog leash.

"Not a single person was marched into a gas chamber and killed."

★ Representative Jeff Miller (R-FL), rebuking a group of Hurricane Katrina survivors at a congressional hearing on December 6, 2005, after they continually likened their temporary housing to concentration camps

The Party's Over

Senate majority whip Mitch McConnell (R-KY) buried a $20 million provision in a 2006 military spending bill "to pay for a celebration in the nation's capital 'for commemoration of success' in Iraq and Afghanistan." But since the United States wasn't successful in Iraq in 2006, the earmarked money surely went back into the general fund, right? Nope, the provision was extended so the president could spend the money in 2007, just in case. Remember that party? Me neither.

"I have seen these liberal psychologists and sociologists talk about there is no need for the man in the family. The woman can take care of the family. It takes a man to provide structure, to provide stability. Not that a woman can't provide stability—I'm not saying that. . . . It does take a father, though."

★ Tom DeLay, in a radio interview with Armstrong Williams, February 10, 2004

Ann Outspoken Conservative

"I'm happy to learn that after I speak you're going to hear from Ann Coulter. That's a good thing. I think it's important to get the views of moderates."

★ Presidential candidate Mitt Romney, referring to conservative writer Ann Coulter at the annual Conservative Political Action Conference on March 2, 2007. During her "moderate" speech, Coulter said, "I was going to have a few comments about John Edwards, but you have to go into rehab if you use the word 'faggot.'" I would hate to see what Romney views as aggressive, wouldn't you?

"I never know what I'm going to say until I say it, so I am kind of interested in hearing what I think."

★ South Carolina state representative John Graham Altman, during an April 2003 debate on a mandatory seatbelt provision

The Letter
of the Law

Representative Jo Ann Emerson (R-MO), in concluding a February 15, 2006, letter written in response to a constituent's complaints about excess oil company profits, wrote: "Once again, thank you for contacting me regarding the testimony of oil company executives before the Senate Commerce Committee. Please feel free to contact me with other matters that are of importance to you. I am honored to serve as your Representative in the U.S. Congress. I think you're an asshole." Wow—an honest politician.

"Fool me once, shame on you. Fool me twice, shame on you."

★ Representative Virginia Foxx (R-NC),
on the House floor, July 21, 2009